YOUR NERVES ARE HAVING

SHOULDER
SURGERY

Neuroscience
Education
for Patients
Having Shoulder
Surgery

Adriaan Louw
PT, PhD

Index

SECTION 1: Your Decision to Have Shoulder Surgery

SECTION 2: Your Alarm System (Your Nervous System)

SECTION 3: Your Nerves and Your Shoulder

SECTION 4: Your Surgery and Your Shoulder Nerves

SECTION 5: Your Nerves Calm Down

SECTION 6: Your Recovery After Shoulder Surgery

SCIENTIFIC SUPPORT FOR YOUR RECOVERY

In each section, you will notice some numbers in the sentences. These numbers refer to scientific articles that support the comments in your booklet. The details of each article are listed at the back of your booklet.

SECTION 1
Your Decision to Have Shoulder Surgery

You have decided to have shoulder surgery. It was likely a big decision, based on test results and response to treatments as well as consultations with your doctor and family. It is important that you do not second-guess yourself. Nobody really "wants" surgery, and the decision to have surgery was likely not easy, but it has been made.[1] Studies have shown that patients who make up their minds and accept that they need to have surgery do better than those who remain unsure.[2,3] Now it is time to move forward, prepare yourself to go through the surgery and work hard on recovery.

Thank you for taking the time to read this booklet. The booklet's goal is to explain what you will experience in the days, weeks and months both before and after your shoulder surgery. Studies have shown that patients who know more about what they can expect do better than those who do not.[4-6] This booklet will provide you with an understanding of how your nerves experience your shoulder pain, surgery and recovery.

You own both your shoulder and your pain. Your surgeon, your physical therapist and your friends and family are there to help you, but _you_ need to take control.

With knowledge and effort, you will be able to do this, and you will help yourself.

Your Alarm System (Your Nervous System)

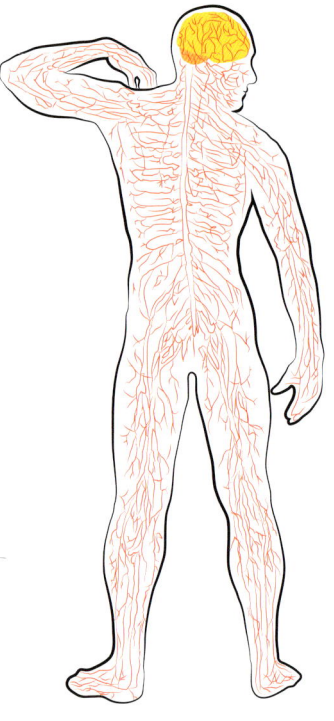

Your nervous system is a continuous structure with all the nerves in your feet, legs, lower back, upper back, arms and neck connected and forming a network like a road system. The main job of your nerves is to monitor your body and to inform you and your brain of anything going on in your body. Some nerves in your body work like an alarm system.[7,8]

Consider when you step on a nail. You want to know about it so you can remove it, get a tetanus shot and not get an infection. The nerves in your foot need to send the message to your brain so that action can be taken. Nerves send messages by using electrical impulses.

At any given time, all nerves have a little bit of electricity running through them. This is normal and shows you are alive.[7,9]

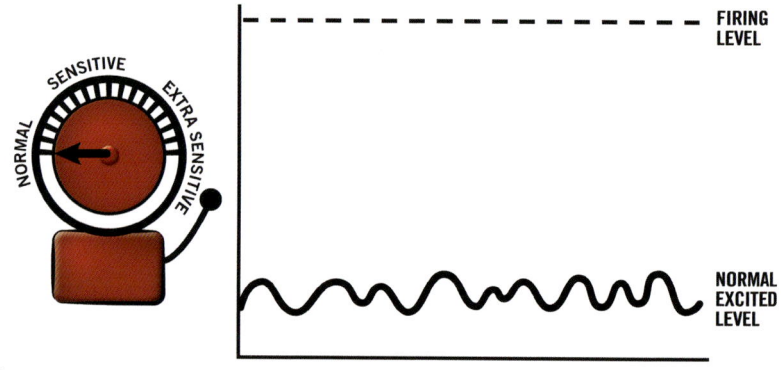

2

When there is danger, such as a nail in the foot, the nerves increase electrical activity and "wake up," sending a lot of danger messages to your spinal cord and ultimately to your brain. They let the brain know there is danger and action is required.[7,9]

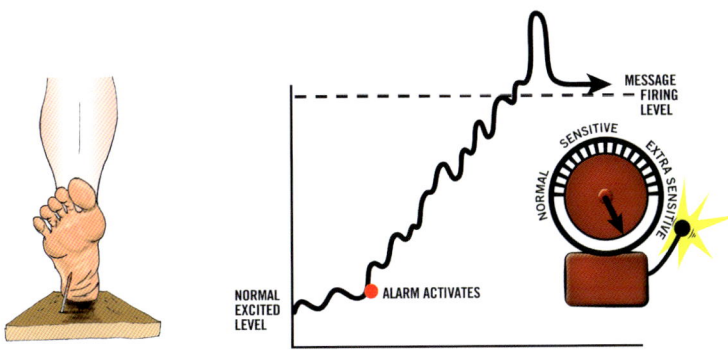

The brain's action may include walking funny, producing stress chemicals in your body or even using a choice word or two.

In this case, it is logical for the brain to produce pain in your foot so that you are alerted to the nail and take action, such as taking the nail out.

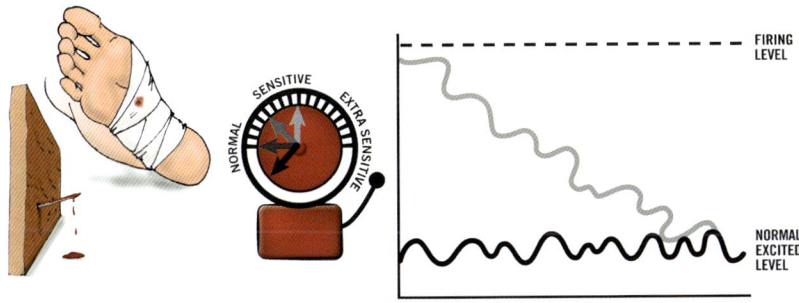

Once you take care of the danger, the nail in this case, it also makes sense for the alarm system to slowly settle down and return to its normal resting level of activity, ready for the next danger.[7,9] You will probably learn to avoid stepping on nails as well.

SECTION 3
Your Nerves and Your Shoulder

Like the nail in the foot, a similar process has occurred in and around your shoulder. Some people are undergoing surgery due to age changes, while others had an injury.[10] As we age, so do our tissues. Aging occurs faster in some people and slower in others, based on our history of joint injury, genetics (mom and dad), jobs and more.[11,12] With the aging there may be increased pain, swelling and inflammation in shoulders with arthritis.[11,12] In other people, an injury may have hurt some tissues in your shoulder.

For the aging shoulders, over time, this low-grade inflammation steadily "woke up" the nerves in and around your shoulder, alerting your brain to the danger in your shoulder. The nerves around the shoulder alerted the spinal cord, which in turn told the brain there is a problem in the shoulder. Similarly, if you had an injury, the nerves around your shoulder "woke up" to alert the brain that there is a problem and you need help.

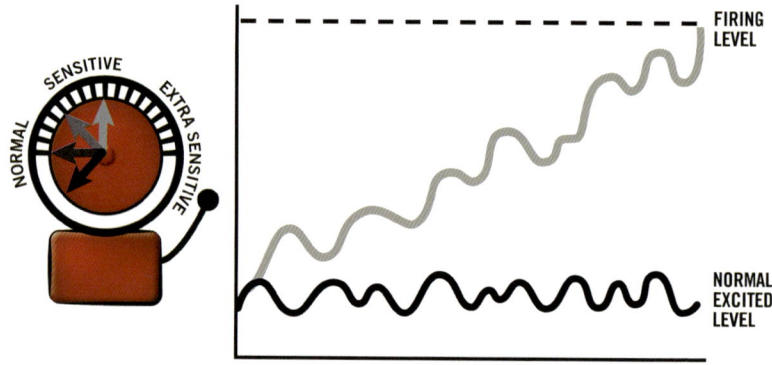

4

THE PAIN CAUSED YOU TO DO THE FOLLOWING:

✓   See your family doctor
✓   See a physical therapist
✓   Have X-rays or an MRI
✓   See a surgeon

In essence, your nerves did their job.

Unlike the "nail in the foot example," when some people's nerves "wake up," they calm down only a little bit and remain elevated and "buzzing."[9,13,14]

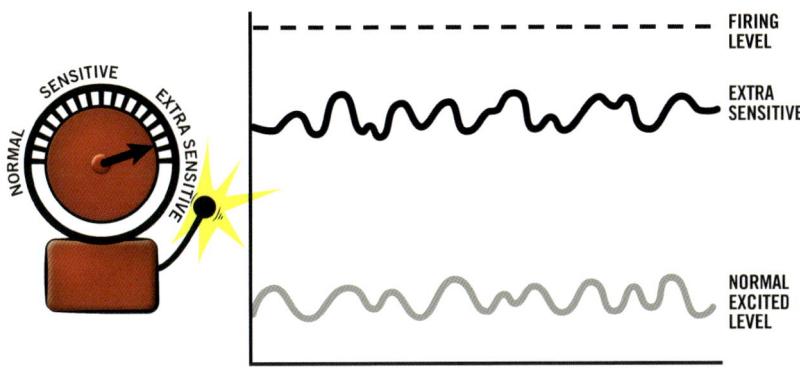

In this state, it does not take much activity, such as movement, carrying things or lying on the shoulder, to make nerves fire off danger messages to the brain.[9,15]

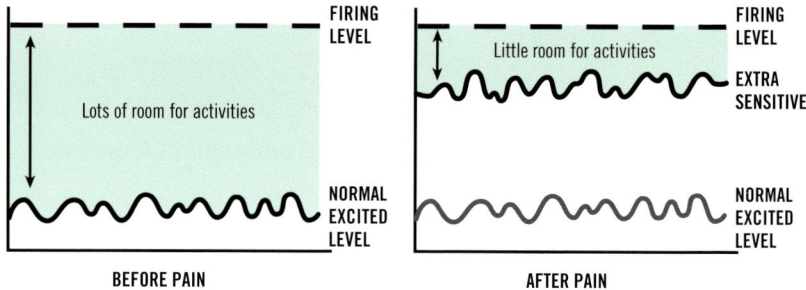

FIRING LEVEL

Lots of room for activities

NORMAL EXCITED LEVEL

BEFORE PAIN

FIRING LEVEL

Little room for activities

EXTRA SENSITIVE

NORMAL EXCITED LEVEL

AFTER PAIN

ANOTHER WAY TO THINK ABOUT YOUR NERVES IS TO COMPARE THEM TO YOUR HOME ALARM SYSTEM.

Imagine an alarm system is set up in your house. Normal day-to-day activities do not set off the alarm. It's set to be sensitive to bigger issues, such as someone breaking a window. Since you have experienced shoulder pain, your alarm system around your shoulder has become so sensitive that when a leaf blows by the house, it sets off the alarm.[15]

Your Nerves and Their Sensors

Your alarm system, however, is the most sophisticated alarm system on the planet. Apart from sending danger messages, your alarm system contains various sensors that are designed to protect and inform you of any changes in your life.[7,8,16]

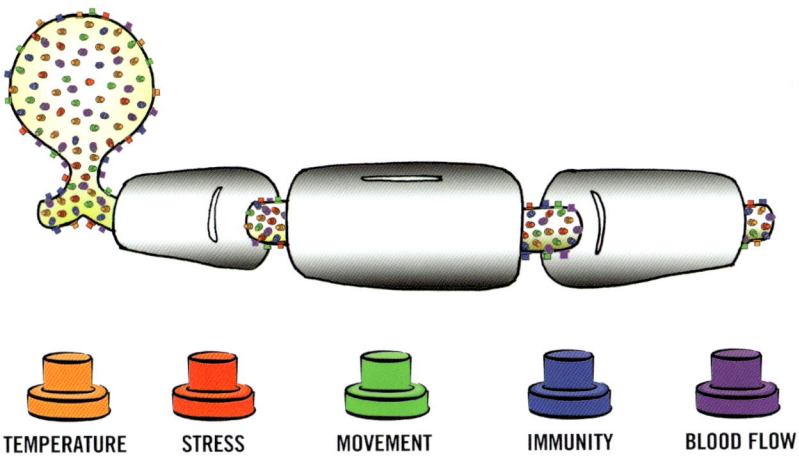

TEMPERATURE   STRESS   MOVEMENT   IMMUNITY   BLOOD FLOW

Various sensors have been identified, but the following may be of particular interest to you:

TEMPERATURE
There are sensors in nerves that tell you if there is a change in temperature. It is not uncommon to become sensitive to cold temperature and feel more aches and pains in the shoulder when it gets cold out. Many people with shoulder arthritis can feel weather changes, which can be explained as your temperature sensors informing you that it's getting cold outside.[7,8,16]

STRESS

There are sensors in nerves that are sensitive to stress chemicals flowing in your blood. The more stressed, anxious, nervous or even upset you are, the more you will experience aches and pains. The more stress chemicals that run through your body, the more stress sensors are activated.[7,8,16]

MOVEMENT AND PRESSURE

There are sensors in your nerves that are sensitive to movement and pressure around them. For example, movement after surgery may activate a few more sensors and make the nerves more sensitive to movement for a little while. A good example would be exercises and physical therapy. Once you move your shoulder and do therapy, the movement sensors around the shoulder will likely "go off" to alert you the shoulder is moving.[7,8,16]

IMMUNITY

When you are sick with the flu, for example, there are many immune molecules floating through your body, helping you deal with the flu. This is the same following shoulder surgery. Recent research shows that when you are really worried and/or have an inflamed body part, you will have an immune response. Nerves have sensors telling them of the increased immune molecules, and the immune chemicals produced can make you ache.[7,8,16]

BLOOD FLOW

There are sensors in your nerves that are sensitive to the amount of blood flowing around your tissues. When blood flow slows down slightly, for example, after sitting too long, these sensors "wake up" and make the nerves sensitive.[7,8,16]

Key points about nerve sensors:

✓ When you developed shoulder pain, your nerves increased their sensitivity to protect you.

✓ This is a normal response.

✓ These sensors change every day based on your thoughts, beliefs and environment.[7,8,16]

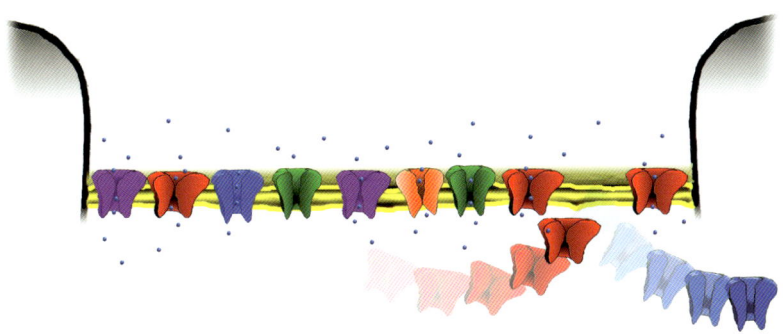

Example: When you face surgery, a little more anxiety is to be expected. In response to the slightly elevated stress chemicals in your blood, nerve sensors wake up, usually in and around the shoulder and arm. You can thus "feel" your shoulder and arm a little more. When stress levels ease, fewer sensors open and your sensitivity decreases.

As mentioned before, nerves are slow to calm down in some people. Why is this? Some people have so many issues surrounding their shoulder pain and surgery that the brain decides it's best to keep the alarm system elevated. Here are some examples:

FAILED TREATMENT

You may begin to wonder why the non-surgical treatment did not work or why the injections helped your neighbor, but not you. You may also wonder if your shoulder will ever get better. As long as your brain has questions and concerns, it will keep your alarm system elevated.[17]

DIFFERENT EXPLANATIONS FOR YOUR PAIN

You can feel more stressed when you have lots of different opinions about your shoulder and what you should be doing.[18] Different opinions will increase some worries and concerns, leaving little incentive for your brain to turn the alarm system down.

FAMILY AND JOB

Since your shoulder pain started, your family life, job and hobbies may have been hijacked by your shoulder pain. This includes endless doctor and therapy visits, expensive tests, lost work time and frustration. In addition, there may be concerns about being able to do your job, the future and money issues. This provides little incentive for the brain to turn the alarm system down.[18]

FEAR

Considering the failed treatments, various opinions, job issues and family concerns, there is likely to be a lot of uncertainty. The uncertainty is usually accompanied by some anxiety or fear. This is quite common, and it has been shown that fear of pain and fear of exercise or movement will keep the alarm system turned on.[19]

Your Nervous System's Neighbors Wake Up

When your nerves in your shoulder "wake up," there are usually some interested neighbors. In Section 2, you learned that your nervous system is connected. Consider the nervous system as an alarm system. If the alarm in your house goes off, it probably wakes the neighbors right next to you. They are curious and concerned about you. If the alarm keeps going, some neighbors down the street may wake up. Nerves work the same way. Since your shoulder and arm alarm systems have been going off for a while, neighboring tissues such as the neck and elbow have likely been awakened.[14] It is not uncommon to experience some sensitivity in your neck as well as the elbow before or after surgery.

Therefore, once you undergo shoulder surgery, it is expected that you may have some remaining pain in the shoulder, arm and neck after the surgery. This is due to the heightened sensitivity of the nerves in the area. This is expected, normal and can easily be explained.

The important issue for you to understand is that your pain may not only be due to the original shoulder issues, but also to the increased sensitivity of the nerves in the region.

Your Surgery and Your Shoulder Nerves

Your surgeon and his or her nurse will explain the procedure for the shoulder surgery. By operating on the shoulder joint, the joint issue (injury, inflammation, swelling and aging) will have been addressed by your surgery.[20,21] Shoulder surgeries have come a long way and are very successful.[20,21]

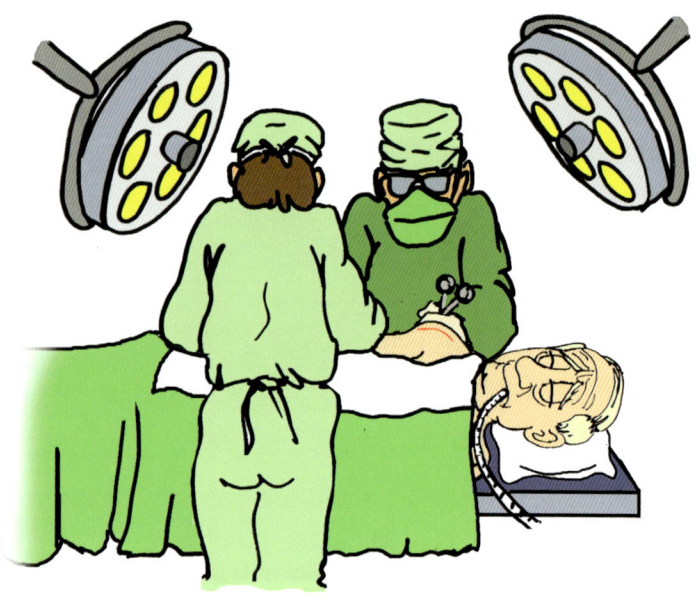

NOW FOR THE IMPORTANT PART:

The surgeon has done his or her job by operating on the shoulder joint. This removes the inflamed joints and tissues, which will no longer irritate the alarm system around the shoulder; your nerves. This is one part of the process. Even though your nerves are not irritated by the inflammation of the joint, they will still be sensitive. The fact that your nerves are still somewhat sensitive after surgery is expected and explained in this booklet.

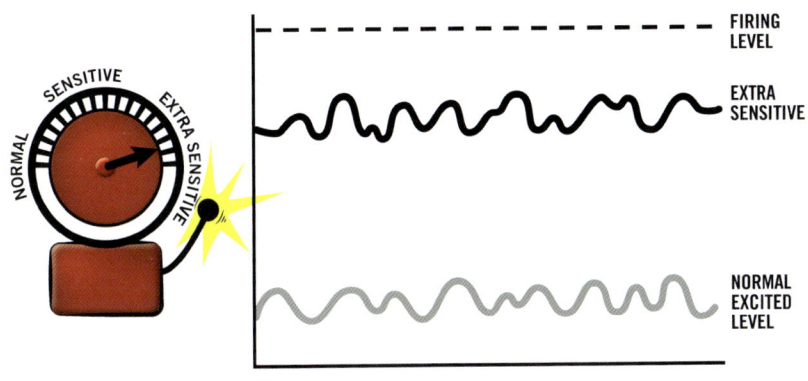

With all the irritation, the nerves are still in "alarm mode." Attention should now focus on calming the nerves down.[15]

Your Hospital Experience, Your Surgery and Your Nerves

It is also important for you to understand that the stress of surgery and the hospital experience may make your nerves even more sensitive in the short term.[22]

HAVING SURGERY

No one wants shoulder surgery unless they really need it. Regardless of the strides made in surgery, such as shorter stays, better surgical methods, and better medications, it is still a stressful time. Anxiety, fear of the unknown and stress will undoubtedly keep your nerves "awake." This is normal. [23,24]

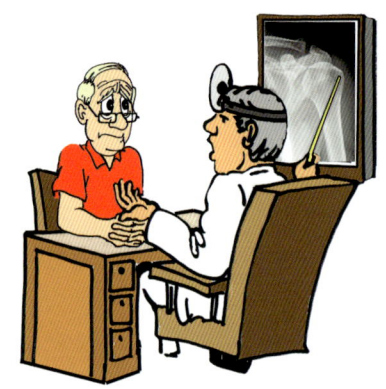

HOSPITAL PROCEDURES

As you prepare for surgery, you need to deal with hospital procedures such as check-in, room assignment and pre-surgical consultation. Unless you are an experienced hospital goer, these procedures may also add to your anxiety.[25]

ANESTHESIA

Undergoing anesthesia for surgery is stressful. As with all the other hospital procedures, it is normal to experience some anxiety in this regard.[26]

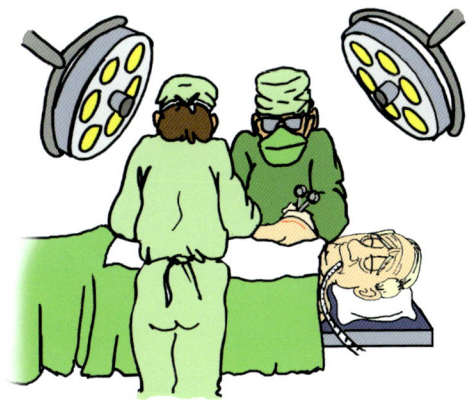

PEOPLE

During your hospitalization, you will deal with many different health care providers. Some you may already know (e.g., family doctor, your surgeon and your surgeon's nurse), while others will be unknown (e.g., floor nurses, operating room personnel, therapists, etc.). There will be a team of people assigned to help you through this process, which may add stress as well.[24]

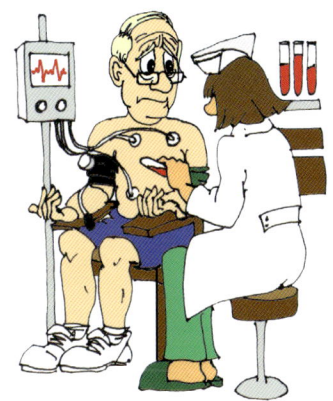

EXPERIENCES

During the hospitalization, pre-anesthesia, surgery and recovery, you will experience various sights and sounds, such as bright lights, tubing and monitors. Although these are all part of the hospital process, they may add additional anxiety.[27]

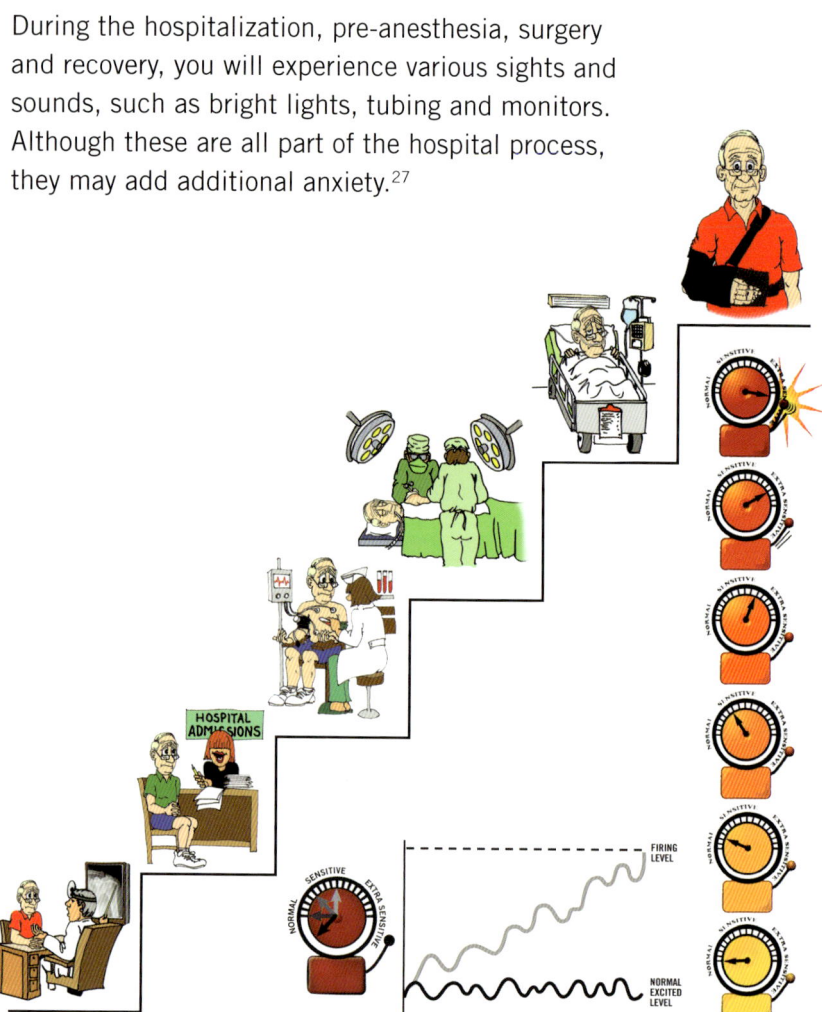

In addition to your nerves having "awakened" due to the shoulder issues, diagnosis and treatment, they will likely be very reactive to the overall surgical experience. Each part of this process may add to a few more alarm signals from the nerves.

SECTION 5
Your Nerves Calm Down

How do we calm nerves down, turn the alarm system down and treat pain? We will discuss three easy steps:

❶ KNOWLEDGE

The good news is you have already started. Research has shown that the more you understand about pain and how it works, the better you will do.[4,28,29] As you read this booklet and gain an increased understanding of the sensitivity of your nerves as part of your pain experience, what you learn actually calms your nerves by turning down the alarm system.[30,31]

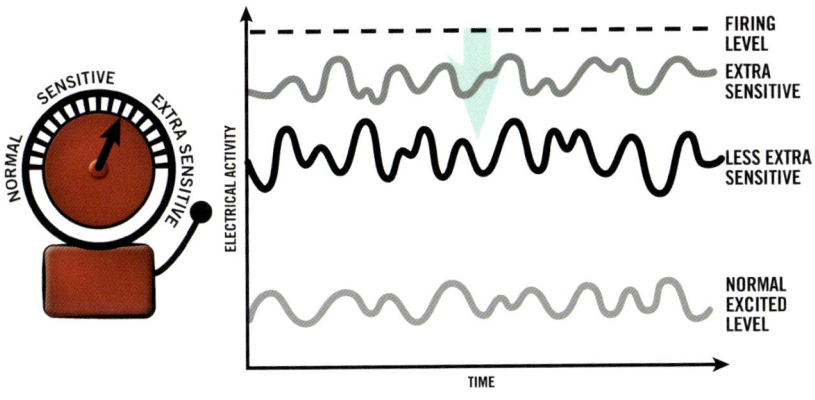

❷ MOVEMENT

Nerves love blood.[32,33] Scientists have shown that when we pump blood and oxygen around nerves, they actually calm down.[33] Exercise that promotes blood flow, such as an aerobic exercise like brisk walking, will help calm your nerves down over time.

Prior to the surgery, do some walking, biking or swimming. After the surgery, your surgeon will ask you to walk to get your lungs working and prevent blood clots. The walking will also help calm your nerves. Biking can also pump blood through the body and calm nerves down. It can even help gain movement of the shoulder.

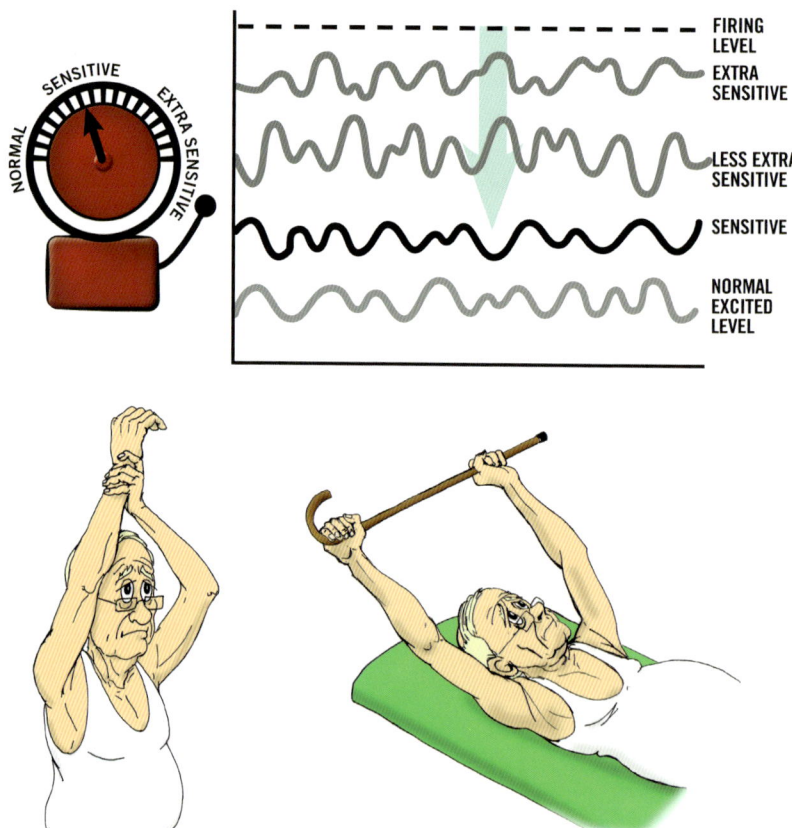

❸ MEDICATION

There are medications designed to calm nerves down.[34] Your surgeon may discuss this with you. You may even be taking them now. Ideally, you will be able to decrease the need for these medications as you recover.

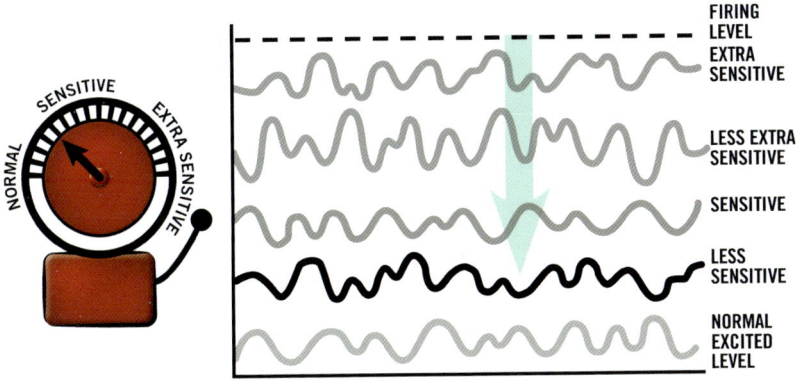

The pain you experience is affected by very powerful chemicals in the brain. Although many people can name five pain medications you can buy over the counter, few know the potent chemicals your brain produces that work like pain medication. The world's most sophisticated and powerful medicine cabinet is situated in your brain.[7,35] The brain uses chemicals such as endorphins, enkephalins, opioids and serotonin to help us ease pain.

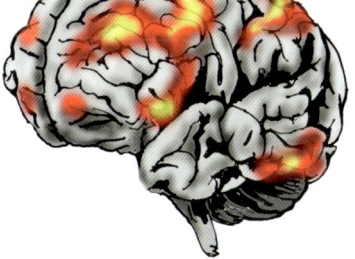

WET BRAIN

A wet brain is the description of a brain with a faucet turned open, flushing pain medication down the spinal cord to dampen incoming danger messages. When you stub your toe, you may experience a lot of pain for a short while. The toe tends to hurt less a few seconds later. In this case, the brain uses these chemicals to ease the pain

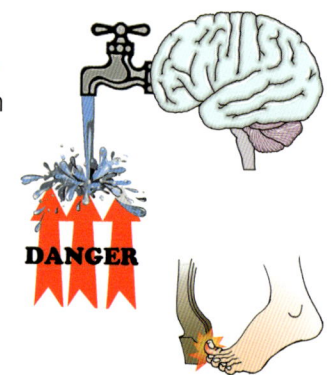

experience. These potent drugs are also used in survival situations and cases where people have serious injuries yet experience little to no pain.[15]

DRY BRAIN

A dry brain is the opposite. In this scenario, the faucet is closed. The longer you experience pain, the less pain medication the brain produces. Although it seems contrary, it is a survival strategy by your brain. Remember that your brain is getting more worried about your shoulder. Because of this, it makes sense to the brain to dry up or close the tap and stop the

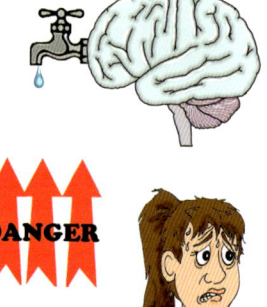

medicine altering the pain experience, urging you to take action.[14]

KNOWLEDGE IS MEDICINE

The more you know about your pain, surgery and nerves, the less worried your brain will be. It will be more likely to turn on the faucet to help turn the alarm system down.

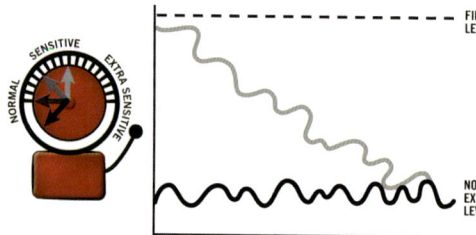

Your Recovery After Shoulder Surgery

✓ Your experiences related to your shoulder and arm pain are normal and can be explained.[4]

✓ Your experiences are stressful and have caused your nerves, your alarm system, to wake up. This is a normal process.[31]

✓ Your pain is real.

✓ Your alarm system is sophisticated. It is unlikely your alarm system will completely turn off immediately, but rather turn down over time.

✓ As your shoulder heals after surgery, you work on recovery and you gain increased understanding of your shoulder and its recovery. The nerve sensitivity will decrease over weeks and months.

✓ Your recovery will have ups and downs, and some flare-ups, which is expected. The flare-ups are not due to harm, but rather due to sensitivity.[14]

✓ Your nerves are barometers for the stresses of life. The more stressed you are, the more shoulder pain you may experience. The calmer you are, the less pain you will experience.

✓ Your recovery requires movement after surgery.[36,37] Your surgeon will give you advice on movement after the operation. As you heal and recover, work on increasing your exercises, movement and walking program. Movement that gets blood and oxygen flowing around your nerves will help calm your nerves down as well as benefit your lungs and general health.

✓ Your medication after surgery will help calm your alarm system.

✓ Medicine also helps the brain produce more of its own pain medication, thus creating a wet brain.

✓ Your doctor and his or her staff, or your physical therapist can help answer any questions you may have. As you should realize by now, the more confused, nervous or uncertain you are, the more sensitive your alarm system will be.

✓ Your hospital stay will be short. In 1-2 weeks you will have a follow-up visit with your surgeon. As time goes on, these post-surgery visits will spread out to coincide with your recovery.

✓ Following your shoulder surgery, you will attend physical therapy to regain your shoulder's movement. Therapy will focus on moving the shoulder, as well as some general strengthening. Remember, your nerves are sensitive and contain movement sensors. You will be aware of the shoulder movements, exercises and stretches, but it does not indicate something is wrong. Your shoulder is just sensitive.

✓ It is important you work on your exercises at home. The harder you work, the faster you will recover and return to regular activities.

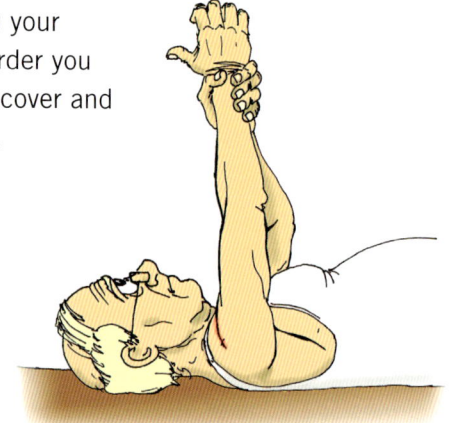

CONCLUSION

Over time, due to aging or from an injury, your shoulder has become painful, swollen and inflamed. This aging process of the joint has also woken up the nerves in and around your shoulder, making them increasingly sensitive. The surgery will correct the joint issues. Following surgery, your nerves around the shoulder will be extra sensitive; this is normal and expected. The more you know about how your nerves work and what causes their sensitivity, the better you will be. Knowledge, gentle movement and realistic goals will help your nerves calm down over time, leading to a successful recovery from shoulder surgery.

Questions For Your Surgeon

Knowledge is power. The more you know about your surgery, the better you will be. Use this page to list questions you want to ask your surgeon.

1 _____

2 _____

3 _____

4 _____

5 _____

Scientific Support for Your Recovery

1. Hawker GA. "Who, when, and why total joint replacement surgery? The patient's perspective." *Current Opinion in Rheumatology*. Sep 2006; 18(5):526-530.
2. Arino Lambea P, Castillo Monsegur J, Sala Serrab M, Cortada Almirall V, Escolano Villen F. "Patients' perception of certainty about decisions to undergo surgery and the relationship between certainty and prior information received". *Revista Espanola de Anestesiologia y Reanimaction*. Oct 2008; 55(8):468-474.
3. Louw A, Butler DS, Diener I, Puentedura EJ. "Development of a preoperative neuroscience educational program for patients with lumbar radiculopathy." *American Journal of Physical Medicine & Rehabilitation/Association of Academic Physiatrists*. May 2013; 92(5):446-452.
4. Louw A, Diener I, Landers MR, Puentedura EJ. "Preoperative pain neuroscience education for lumbar radiculopathy: a multicenter randomized controlled trial with 1-year follow-up." *Spine*. Aug 15 2014; 39(18):1449-1457.
5. Louw A, Diener I, Puentedura EJ. "The short term effects of preoperative neuroscience education for lumbar radiculopathy: A case series." *International Journal of Spine Surgery*. 2015; 9:11.
6. Yee A, Adjei N, Do J, Ford M, Finkelstein J. "Do patient expectations of spinal surgery relate to functional outcome?" *Clinical Orthopaedics and Related Research*. May 2008; 466(5):1154-1161.
7. Louw A, Puentedura E. *Therapeutic Neuroscience Education: Teaching Patients about Pain*. Minneapolis, MN: OPTP; 2013.
8. Butler DS, Moseley GL. *Explain Pain*. 2nd Ed. Adelaide, Australia: NOI Publishing; 2013.
9. Louw A, Zimney K, O'Hotto C, Hilton S. "The clinical application of teaching people about pain." *Physiotherapy Theory and Practice*. Jul 2016; 32(5):385-395.
10. Bodin J, Ha C, Chastang JF, et al. "Comparison of risk factors for shoulder pain and rotator cuff syndrome in the working population." *American Journal of Industrial Medicine*. Jul 2012; 55(7):605-615.
11. Milgrom C, Schaffler M, Gilbert S, van Holsbeeck M. "Rotator-cuff changes in asymptomatic adults. The effect of age, hand dominance and gender." *The Journal of Bone and Joint Surgery*. British volume. Mar 1995; 77(2):296-298.
12. Sher JS, Uribe JW, Posada A, Murphy BJ, Zlatkin MB. "Abnormal findings on magnetic resonance images of asymptomatic shoulders." *The Journal of Bone and Joint Surgery*. American volume. Jan 1995; 77(1):10-15.
13. Bedson J, Croft PR. "The discordance between clinical and radiographic knee osteoarthritis: a systematic search and summary of the literature." *BMC Musculoskeletal Disorders*. 2008; 9:116.
14. Woolf CJ, Mannion RJ. "Neuropathic pain: aetiology, symptoms, mechanisms, and management." *The Lancet*. Jun 5 1999; 353(9168):1959-1964.
15. Louw A. *Why Do I Hurt? A Patient Book about the Neuroscience of Pain*. Minneapolis: OPTP; 2013.
16. Devor M. "The pathophysiology of damaged peripheral nerves." *Wall & Melzack's Textbook of Pain*. 3rd ed. Edinburgh: Churchill Livingstone; 1994.
17. Cleland JA, Fritz JM, Brennan GP. "Predictive validity of initial fear avoidance beliefs in patients with low back pain receiving physical therapy: is the FABQ a useful screening tool for identifying patients at risk for a poor recovery?" *European Spine Journal*. Jan 2008; 17(1):70-79.
18. Kendall NAS, Linton SJ, Main CJ. "Guide to assessing psychosocial yellow flags in acute low back pain: risk factors for long term disability and work loss." Wellington: Accident Rehabilitation & Compensation Insurance Corporation of New Zealand and the National Health Committee; 1997.

19. Vlaeyen JW, Linton SJ. "Fear-avoidance and its consequences in chronic musculoskeletal pain: a state of the art." *Pain*. Apr 2000; 85(3):317-332.
20. Chaudhury S, Gwilym SE, Moser J, Carr AJ. "Surgical options for patients with shoulder pain." *Nature Reviews Rheumatology*. Apr 2010; 6(4):217-226.
21. Coghlan JA, Buchbinder R, Green S, Johnston RV, Bell SN. "Surgery for rotator cuff disease." *The Cochrane Database of Systematic Reviews*. Jan 23 2008(1):CD005619.
22. Louw A, Diener I, Butler DS, Puentedura EJ. "Preoperative education addressing postoperative pain in total joint arthroplasty: review of content and educational delivery methods." *Physiotherapy Theory and Practice*. Apr 2013; 29(3):175-194.
23. Rice M, Glasper A, Keeton D, Spargo P. "The effect of a preoperative education programme on perioperative anxiety in children: an observational study." *Paediatric Anaesthesia*. May 2008; 18(5):426-430.
24. Rosen S, Svensson M, Nilsson U. "Calm or not calm: the question of anxiety in the perianesthesia patient." *Journal of PeriAnesthesia Nursing*. Aug 2008; 23(4):237-246.
25. Walker JA. "Emotional and psychological preoperative preparation in adults." *British Journal of Nursing*. Apr 25-May 8 2002; 11(8):567-575.
26. McEwen A, Moorthy C, Quantock C, Rose H, Kavanagh R. "The effect of videotaped preoperative information on parental anxiety during anesthesia induction for elective pediatric procedures." *Paediatric Anaesthesia*. Jun 2007; 17(6):534-539.
27. Yeh ML, Chen HH, Liu PH. "Effects of multimedia with printed nursing guide in education on self-efficacy and functional activity and hospitalization in patients with hip replacement." *Patient Education and Counseling*. May 2005; 57(2):217-224.
28. Louw A, Zimney K, Puentedura EJ, Diener I. "The efficacy of pain neuroscience education on musculoskeletal pain: A systematic review of the literature." *Physiotherapy Theory and Practice*. Jul 2016; 32(5):332-355.
29. Moseley GL, Hodges PW, Nicholas MK. "A randomized controlled trial of intensive neurophysiology education in chronic low back pain." *Clinical Journal of Pain*. 2004; 20:324-330.
30. Moseley GL. "Widespread brain activity during an abdominal task markedly reduced after pain physiology education: fMRI evaluation of a single patient with chronic low back pain." *Australian Journal of Physiotherapy*. 2005; 51(1):49-52.
31. Louw A, Puentedura EJ, Diener I, Peoples RR. "Preoperative therapeutic neuroscience education for lumbar radiculopathy: a single-case fMRI report." *Physiotherapy Theory and Practice*. 2015; 31(7):496-508.
32. Butler DS. *The Sensitive Nervous System*. Adelaide: Noigroup; 2000.
33. Kuphal KE, Fibuch EE, Taylor BK. "Extended swimming exercise reduces inflammatory and peripheral neuropathic pain in rodents." *The Journal of Pain*. Dec 2007; 8(12):989-997.
34. Yu L, Ran B, Li M, Shi Z. "Gabapentin and pregabalin in the management of postoperative pain after lumbar spinal surgery: a systematic review and meta-analysis." *Spine*. Oct 15 2013; 38(22):1947-1952.
35. Gifford L. *Aches and Pains*. Cornwall: WordPress; 2014.
36. Boissonnault WG, Badke MB, Wooden MJ, Ekedahl S, Fly K. "Patient outcome following rehabilitation for rotator cuff repair surgery: the impact of selected medical comorbidities." *The Journal of Orthopaedic and Sports Physical Therapy*. Jun 2007; 37(6):312-319.
37. Brennan GP, Parent EC, Cleland JA. "Description of clinical outcomes and postoperative utilization of physical therapy services within 4 categories of shoulder surgery." *The Journal of Orthopaedic and Sports Physical Therapy*. Jan 2010; 40(1):20-29.

More patient books by Adriaan Louw

These neuroscience education books use simple language to help you understand and lessen your pain. Concepts are explained using memorable metaphors, and strategies are provided to calm your nervous system and reduce pain. Written by therapist Adriaan Louw, available exclusively from OPTP. Learn more at **OPTP.com**.

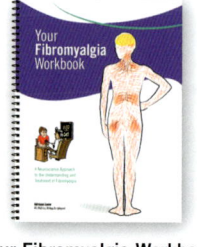

Your Fibromyalgia Workbook
ITEM #8747

Why Do I Hurt? Workbook
ITEM #8756

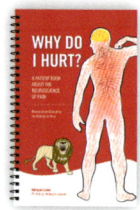

Why Do I Hurt?
ITEM #8746

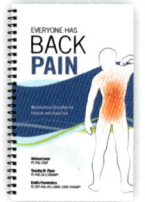

Everyone Has Back Pain
ITEM #8754

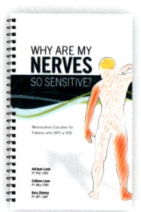

Why Are My Nerves So Sensitive?
ITEM #8752

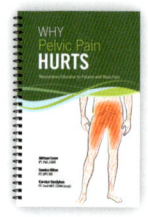

Why Pelvic Pain Hurts
ITEM #8742

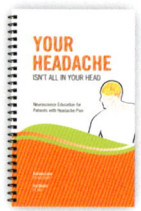

Your Headache Isn't All In Your Head
ITEM #8749

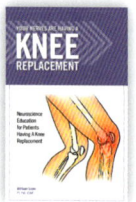

Your Nerves Are Having A Knee Replacement
ITEM #8753

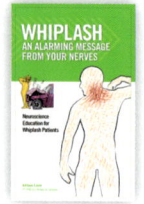

Whiplash: An Alarming Message
ITEM #8744

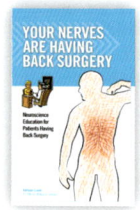

Your Nerves Are Having Back Surgery
ITEM #8745